Published by Jennifer Topper

Happy Cooking

D1518980

The Un-Cookbook

Introduction: How To Read This Book

Unlike traditional cookbooks, this one does not contain hundreds of recipes. Instead, my objective is to enable you to prepare delicious meals without the crutch of a recipe—most of which are written with the assumption that the reader already knows an enormous amount of cooking basics. I've noticed that there are just too many variables impacting the outcome of a recipe attempted as it is written on the page. The limitations of cooking by recipes take away from the passion and fun of cooking intuitively. I've always felt that preparing food could be an adventure, like exploring a part of town you've never been to before, or traveling to a far-away destination. Food is not math—the outcome will most likely not be the exact same each time you replicate a recipe (I'm sure I'll have some pastry chefs quarrelling with that claim), whether it is done from a written recipe or if is from your own memory. It can be an art, even though you only have 10 minutes to pull together appetizers and drinks for a surprise visit from your in-laws.

Everyone has intuition when it comes to food: if you have taste buds, you have intuition! You can cook a great dish without measuring carefully or following a written recipe to the letter. You can intuitively "forage" in your pantry and pull together a great meal of leftovers or arcane ingredients you've never used before. If you know what you like and you taste what you are cooking often, you are cooking intuitively. Welcome to the world of cooking like a chef...or your grandmother!

This book is not about being a hack. Sure, there are shortcuts, tricks and ways to cut corners that every hack in a kitchen knows about. But for the everyday cook who doesn't have the time, the training, the resources, or the money to prepare elaborate meals, I'd like to equip you with some fundamental tenets:

- **Simplicity**
- **Quality**
- **Taste**

Chapter 1 Basic Basics

My Pantry, Your Pantry

Planning, Timing

"Mise-en-Place"

Your Tools

Salt, Fat, Sweet, Zesty

Demystifying Cooking Terms like *Deglazing, Reductions*

Vegetables Are Your Friend

Making a Lot out of a Little: Presentation and Foraging

Quick tips

Chapter 2 Start from the Start

Vinaigrettes and Dressings

Salads like you never knew salads

Snacks, Appetizers, Party foods

Chapter 3 Demystify Soups, Sauces, Stews

Life Without Cans

Soup Base

Tomato Sauce

Chapter 4   Dessert

What more is there to say—it's dessert

Chapter 1

Basic Basics

This book does not look like your typical recipe book. I wouldn't write a cookbook because every recipe anyone ever needs is probably already written somewhere—they're just not written for everybody. It is not the recipes that this book is about, it is about the style and intuition of cooking. You must be truly interested in cooking good food! This book is not a quickie-guide-to-quickie-4-star-meals, but it is a good start to a lifetime of gratification from making great food.

Most cookbooks are written with the assumption that the reader-cook already understands the intentions or certain basics about cooking. There are easier ways to guide people to cook successfully, and I've found that a step-by-step from the start will encourage great kitchen habits and cultivate a true sense of intuitive cooking from the onset. If my husband can cook braised short-ribs in Barolo with caramelized root vegetables from a one-page, 11-step e-mail I sent to him, you can, too.

On the whole, I've pulled together some of the keys to successful, intuitive cooking that have guided me for years that I'd like to share with you:

I like to cook without rules (I like to do everything without rules, but we'll stick with cooking for now.) Rigidity and inflexibility can lead to a disaster in the kitchen, except for those few professional chefs who must stick to rules and limitations to keep their customers coming back for consistency's sake. I am interested in spreading the optimistic word that everyone can be a great cook, if we just learn how to taste. Cooking is about tasting. With a few adjustments that are simpler than you can imagine, that bland soup or that cardboard pot roast can usually be fixed...and with a much simpler resolution than you thought! So don't throw it out without trying to fix it or use it for another purpose! Maybe your soup came out so thick and dense you just can't serve it as a soup—will it work as a dip for homemade crackers if you add it to some pureed white beans? Will it work as a sauce or marinade for a pork roast? Don't give up on it!

I never waste anything. Nearly every morsel can be used or re-applied for another purpose. The inedible pumpkin brownies that you *intuitively* did not think would work, but you tried the recipe anyway because the cookbook said they would be great, can actually turn into something wonderful once you free yourself from thinking that these brownies must be served as brownies. Crumble them up and toast them to use as sprinkles on vanilla ice cream instead. And if *that* doesn't work, then trash them. But open your mind, first, and don't be afraid of trying something different. However, remember that yucky ingredients make yucky food.

Good cooking is simplicity. I worked with a great chef who professed to using only 3 main ingredients in each dish (this doesn't include pantry items, seasoning, and your obvious basic things like onions or garlic or olive oil or salt). This is a school of thought that does not lend itself to the complex, laundry-list of ingredients that you may find on your local fusion restaurant menu. But it is also a school of thought that has led me to cook wonderful meals under tight circumstances or on a very limited budget. I can't tell you how easy it is to make tomato sauce that is healthy, quick, and simple. Why bother spending $5 on a can or bottle of sauce with mystery ingredients, sugars, preservatives, and added garbage that you find you must re-season before you put it on your pasta, anyway?

I use fresh, local ingredients that are in season. Use good-tasting ingredients. I'd like to address one problem I see in dozens of kitchens: *a great way to get rid of a bad wine is to cook with it.* WRONG!! A bad wine is going to cook down into a bad sauce. The same goes for all ingredients in your dishes. Use beautiful, fresh apples for your apple pie—don't use those chalky, beat-up apples that have been sitting in your fridge for weeks. They will taste as nasty cooked as they would uncooked, so get rid of them or put them in your mulch pile. Use your judgment with vegetables, as well. All too frequently carrots don't taste sweet or celery tastes metallic. Taste your basic ingredients before you put them into a pot, because even if they are to stew for hours, it won't erase an inherently gross taste or texture.

Learn how to taste. One of the toughest things about your journey to learning about your own ability to cook intuitively will be learning how to taste. You'll want to *deconstruct* your food tasting—in other words, back-in to the intuitive cooking process. Start by tasting your soups, sauces, and salads before you venture into cooking and figure out what makes them good! They are salty, sweet, balanced, and don't need fixing before you jump into your meal. Food that comes out of your kitchen should already be well-seasoned, so that your guest (or yourself) will not need to pour on the salt or chili flakes at the table.

The difficulty in overcoming your seasoning ability will be to realize how much salt you'll be using (and in some cases, fat. Do you know why grilled cheese sandwiches taste so much better at the diner? Fat). In addition, the various flavors (and the tasty fat) felt on each side of your tongue work together in mysterious ways…the balance of acidic, sweet, salty, and bitter. Although this seems like a science, it is more of an art in how you can accomplish the tasting, then the cooking. You will integrate this balance when you cook—everything from the simplest oil and vinegar salad dressing to a more complex soup or sauce.

Baking is more of a science, in my opinion. Intuitive cooking in baking will require a more strict interpretation of a recipe because of the chemistry of how eggs function as a leavener, how flour can be overworked to become too glutinous (a tough dough), and how sugar, butter, yeast and other leaveners work together. But it doesn't mean you can't add some chocolate to your favorite pound cake recipe, or change up the fruit in a crostata or cake recipe. For example, I use one basic cookie dough recipe and swap in the flavors depending on my mood or the occasion—lemon, chocolate chip, almond, pignoli-licorice.

But it's not rocket science. People aren't *born* with cooking abilities! You will fall on your face with some losing recipes, but don't be discouraged. Step back and simplify your efforts, plan your meal, and plot out where you're going. You'll probably do great every time! But keep in mind, there may be some things that you just can't do the way you want to. I still can't make my perfect grilled cheese, seriously. Don't get hung up on it—if you can't get it the first few times, try a different recipe and move on. Remember—be flexible!!

Basic Definitions

✓ When I mention **roasting** or **baking** something in the oven, assume it is as a pre-heated temperature of about 350 degrees. (This also means that before you put something in the oven to cook, it's good to have it already heated.) **Bake** is the setting you will use for roasting, heating through, and baking, and that heat originates from the bottom and heats the entire oven.

✓ **Saute**. This is not a hoity-toity word, believe me. All this means is putting some food in a pan with a bit of oil or butter and cooking it. That's it. No brain surgery. Things you want to pay attention to, however, the heat under your pan. You don't want to scorch foods that are meant to gradually cook with a bit of browning.

✓ **Browning.** Brown on food that doesn't come that way generally means that you've cooked some of the water out of it and the brown part is the sugars in the food (not necessarily any sugar that you've added, but the natural sugars) have *caramelized.* Brown bits in a pan generally mean flavor, albeit ugly, and could be used to enhance the flavor of a sauce, soup, stew or gravy by simply *deglazing* with a liquid and scraping up those bits.

✓ **Broil.** Your oven has two settings: broil and bake. Broil is the heat or gas flame originates from the top and is meant to brown foods quickly. Really quickly.

✓ Terms that I won't be using include some you see in restaurants. *Pan-searing* means cooking something (generally a fish or meat) at a high temperature in a pan for a short time…it is the definition of searing, too, so the *pan* part is superfluous. Same with *oven-roasting*—where else would you roast it? Your open fire pit?

✓ **The Most Important Point, Before You Read Any Further:** Season your food!! Use salt! Don't be afraid! Even if it is not mentioned in a recipe, just about every single recipe requires seasoning with salt, sugar, acid, and more salt. So be mindful that you must salt your meat before you put it on the grill; salt your onions and garlic before sautéing; sweeten your blueberries before you put them in your pie crust.

Don't get your **Pantries** in a bunch

Be sentimental and reconnect with your pantry! Get to know the bottles, boxes, and cans hidden in the dark corners of your cabinets. If it is more than one year old, get your trash bin ready for a workout. Start fresh and clean out the old stuff! But don't throw out those things you just don't know about. Keep the saffron, and keep that weird can of truffled foie gras you got in your Christmas stocking. But get rid of spice containers that were there when you moved in. Here's what I always keep in my pantry, and you should, too:

✓ **Cans of Beans.** Canellini (white beans), chick peas, black beans, pinto beans. Beans are a beautiful and versatile protein. They are a filler for soups, they are wonderful in salads, drop them into a steaming bowl of barley, and blend them for a wonderful (and low-fat) dip for crackers and cheese.

✓ **Cans of Tuna (frankly, I prefer Sardines and they contain less mercury)** Always a great way to make a boring pasta dish interesting, same goes for a salad. Forget the mayo! Canned fish is a beautiful thing with batches of olive oil, vinegar, capers, chopped red onions and a handful of fresh (or dried) herbs and salt & pepper. Serve with boiled potatoes and extra virgin olive oil as an antepasti!

✓ **Whole, peeled canned San Marzano Tomatoes.** Hey, it's not summer year-round, and you need your tomatoes for sauces, soups, and stews!

✓ **Different Vinegars.** Balsamic, Red Wine, Champagne, Cider, infused, Rice Wine...any flavors are wonderful. Just move your white vinegar under the sink to serve the purpose of unclogging your drain...white vinegar is not worthy of food, but it does a great job cleaning your windows.

✓ **Asian Flavors.** This is vague, I know. Just a sampling includes soy sauce and tamari, rice wine and rice wine vinegar, hoisin sauce, plum sauce, black bean sauce, sriracha, red curry, peanut oil, sesame oil. Believe it or not, you can flavor a regular batch of spaghetti into a great bowl of Asian noodles with peanut butter, sesame oil, and soy sauce. Seriously, read on.

✓ **Nuts and Seeds.** Generally I like to keep nuts in the fridge, they won't get rancid and they stay fresher that way. Walnuts, almonds, pine nuts (pignolis), flax seeds, sunflower seeds, pumpkin seeds are staples for salads, mixed with yogurt, in rice or pasta. Give it a shot.

- ✓ **Kosher Salt.** No, we're not keeping a kosher or halal kitchen. But kosher salt, as it is called, is the big chunky salt that is best to cook with. You get a better feel for how much you are adding when you feel it between your fingers!

- ✓ **Flour.** Not just for baking, it could be used for thickening sauces or soups (as a last resort!), for dusting shrimp or pork chops before frying or sautéing, for making fresh pasta!

- ✓ **"Condiments."** Mustard, horseradish, pickled ginger, ketchup, all can be used as emulsifiers (we'll get to that in the next chapter) for salad dressings, marinades or crusts.

- ✓ **Chili flakes, Tabasco, pepper.** Never underestimate the beauty of heat. Just when you least expected that tangy bite…

- ✓ **Onions, potatoes, garlic.** Speak for themselves.

- ✓ **Canned* Chicken broth.** Not just for soup anymore! You can *deglaze* (in a later chapter) your sauté pan, make a much tastier bowl of rice or grains, use in mashed potatoes if you don't feel like fattening up on butter, milk or sour cream. It can be a lifesaver! *Later on in the **Soup** chapter I'll show you that you can make your own chicken and vegetable broth for long term storage in your freezer in a snap.

- ✓ **Frozen Peas.** Perfect year-round, they are a great thing to have on hand if you have NOTHING left to eat in the house except some penne and an old hunk of parmesan. They wake up soups, they are fun to eat in salads, they work well in the old leftover favorite, shepherd's pie (smashed potatoes layered with ground beef, onions and peas).

- ✓ **Spices.** Don't go crazy with spices, especially until you are more comfortable and confident in your seasoning. Plus, you can go a lifetime without needing allspice. Grocery stores now sell fresh spices year-round in cute little plastic containers in the produce section, so go with that whenever you can. *Always try to buy whole spices and grind them…also, you'll want to toast spices before grinding to let out the essential oils. Sprinkle those seeds in a dry pan on a medium flame and shake the pan for a minute or two until you smell the spice, and then take off the heat immediately.* Some dried spices I find myself using frequently include

  - ○ **Herbes de Provence** (a blend of herbs from France)

  - ○ **Ras al Hanout** (a Middle Eastern blend generally consisting of sumac, paprika, cumin, coriander, turmeric, ginger, nutmeg, mace, fennel)

- ○ **Whole Seeds** (reserve your coffee grinder to grind whole spices): cumin, coriander, fennel/anise

And that's it. Like I said, you won't need tons of spices to season your dishes—stick with fresh ingredients, enough salt, and a balance of sweet and acidic, and you'll be good to go most of the time.

Planning, Timing

You will love how organized you'll become. Part of what makes us crazy in the kitchen is that we don't plan enough in advance. I'm not talking about sitting down for a several hours plotting out every move before you microwave some ramen noodles and open a Coke. I'm talking about stopping for a moment before you turn on your stove and preparing what you will need for your little journey in making this meal. You will see in these recipes that the bulk of the work comes in the planning stages of making a meal—not the actual cooking itself since I tend to make one-pot meals with very few ingredients. Once you've planned, you'll fly through your cooking endeavor seamlessly! Whether you are making Friday night dinner for you and your dog alone, or you are putting together Thanksgiving for 20, you need to stop and think about what you are doing before you jump into the chopping and pre-heating part. Take my word: Things get burned when you are not organized.

Here is a Checklist

- ✓ Clean up your preparation area. Move the bills, sunglasses, keys and toys away from your cooking area

- ✓ Think about (or write down) everything you are going to need for your cooking endeavor and put all these pieces on your counter before you even think about touching your oven or stovetop

- ✓ Take out all of your tools you will need (see Your Tools, next)—your paring knife, your chef's knife, your tongs, your peeler, your pan, your strainer in the sink, etc. so you don't run around your kitchen flailing like a lunatic looking for your whisk while your sauce is burning

- ✓ Take out all of the ingredients you will be using for your meal and unwrap, untie, open the can and measure out, chop up and prepare everything you will need before you even think about turning on the stove

This way, you won't be throwing things around wildly looking for something while your main dish is burning on the stove!

Timing is important.

Example:

Brunch with your in-laws is at 11am—don't go out jogging at 10am without your prep work out of the way. Here is an example of how you would organize yourself: Make the coffee first, get it out of the way. What can you do that won't get cold or yucky earlier in the morning—

cut up the fruit and macerate the fruit salad (add some chopped fresh mint and a few swigs or rum or Grand Marnier); make the pancake batter and refrigerate; Arrange the smoked salmon on the plate, slice the lemons, tomatoes and chop the parsley and cover in the fridge. Set the table and arrange the flowers the night before. Crack the eggs for scrambling and set them in a bowl in the fridge. Soften the butter on the counter so it'll be delightfully spreadable for the toast!

Here is a Checklist

✓ Defrosting takes a really long time—do not expect to eat it for dinner tonight if the turkey breast in the freezer isn't defrosting in the fridge by yesterday morning

✓ DO put the water on to boil for your pasta while you chop your onions, garlic, and herbs and crush your canned tomatoes in a separate bowl for marinara sauce, but;

✓ DON'T start sautéing your fish before you've chopped the vegetables for your salad and prepared your vinaigrette, roasted your potatoes, or put the cobbler in the oven. It will burn...see what I mean?

✓ Try to go shopping for produce and meat no earlier than a day or two before you plan on serving. Even if it's more convenient to go shopping on Tuesday for your Sunday night dinner with Mom and Dad, you're much better off with fresher food. It will taste better and you won't spend as much time picking out the nasty, mushy leaves from your mesclun mix.

✓ Use timers. Write lists. No one becomes Julia Child overnight—and she had assistants.

"Mise-en-Place"

Along the lines of what we've been talking about with planning and timing, your Mise-en-Place is the French culinary term for your prepped ingredients before you even turn on the heat. I can't emphasize enough how important it is that you prepare your ingredients in advance of cooking them. For a multi-course meal or a party, you will probably use one ingredient in a number of places. *It doesn't take that long!* For example:

✓ Dice your onion to sauté the liver, and slice the onion to caramelize for the roasted potatoes: work with all your onions at once, so you don't need to re-wash your cutting board and lose valuable time crying over the same onion twice!

- ✓ While you're in chopping mode, get your parsley, chives, and basil out of the way at once and stash them in their own containers for use later.
- ✓ Once you've planned your meal and you identify what ingredients you will need
- ✓ Set out the herbs you plan on using so that you aren't running through your kitchen to find a container.
- ✓ Take everything you will need out on a countertop so that you don't forget to prep or cook something you had initially planned.
- ✓ Wash off and clean your meat or fish and set on a clean plate ready for roasting/sautéing/braising
- ✓ Open containers, cans, or boxes that may cause a little frazzle later on when you are running around: to avoid cuts, spills, and rampant cursing

Your Tools

I once knew a guy who used a barbeque set of tools in his tiny, downtown New York studio apartment kitchen. Nothing was funnier or clumsier than seeing him stir a pot of rice & beans with a 2-foot spatula with a giant wooden handle. My roommate in college used an old Jiffy-Pop popcorn aluminum container as her ad hoc pan for grilled cheeses. To this day, my friend only buys variety-packs of cereal because he cuts through the back of each individual child-size box and pours milk right in it so that he doesn't have to use a bowl—because he owns no bowls. On the other hand, my aunt has never stepped foot in her kitchen and, yet, owns an All-Clad (e.g., *very, very expensive and high-quality)* pot and pan set, and is outfitted with tools to make a pro-chef wither with envy.

You see what I'm getting at?

If you are planning on cooking decent, tasty, healthy meals every now and then, please equip yourself with the tools so that you can accomplish your goals without struggling. You don't need to spend thousands; but please don't re-use Chinese take-out containers to steam vegetables in your microwave and serve to your spouse's boss…too much can go wrong there! You can buy unfashionable but very functional and durable cooking tools at a restaurant supply store for less money than the department stores. Plus, restaurant supply stores are barrels of fun.

Here's a Checklist

- ✓ 10-inch Chef's Knife, 7-inch boning knife, set of sharp paring knives. *KEEP YOUR KNIVES SHARP—IT WILL ABSOLUTELY MAKE ALL THE DIFFERENCE IN THE WORLD. I guarantee it.*

- ✓ 1 no-stick pan (not an omelette pan, you don't need a special pan to make omelettes). Do not put it in the dishwasher, use only silicone or wood utensils, and replace it every 4 months or so

- ✓ Big pot, small pot, braising pot (Not non-stick, because you will only scrape it)

- ✓ Tongs

- ✓ Large serving spoons: 1 slotted (with holes), 1 without; ladle

- ✓ Measuring cups and pyrex 2-cup measure

- ✓ Roasting pan—I prefer ceramic if you only want to buy one

- ✓ Non-stick cookie sheet

- ✓ Springform cake pan

- ✓ Vegetable peeler

- ✓ Colander (large bowl-like looking thing with holes in it) and small strainer (smaller screen-like looking thing with handle)

- ✓ Blender/Cuisinart and/or Immersion blender

- ✓ Set of kitchen/mixing bowls—large and small

- ✓ A few durable cutting boards: plastic can be put in the dishwasher

Salt, Fat, Sweet, Zesty

Salt. Somehow, salt works wonders with flavors. I'm not a scientist or a chemist, so I can't tell you why. But if a dish seems like it's missing something, go for the salt to season it, first. Amply salt your meats and fish before grilling, roasting or cooking. Salt your veggies before sautéing so that they can *sweat* out excess water and *caramelize* tastefully. I use salted butter when baking (ever notice in recipes that they say to use unsalted butter, yet the recipe calls for salt?), just to save a step in measuring out salt, but you will meet experienced bakers who would call me a hack for that. Use more salt than you think you should. You'll be using Kosher Salt from now on, so get used to it! Sea Salt is your friend—pick up a fancy container of sea salt and sprinkle on your finished dish.

Fat is flavor. Every chef knows this, which is why eating in restaurants is generally quite fattening because you'd be shocked at how much fat is used to make those tasty foods so tasty. Butter, oil, cream, olive oil, lard, rendered fat—it's all delicious when used in food, we can't deny it. However, we don't need to use so much fat at home to cook delicious foods.

✓ Fat functions as lubrication in your pan so your vegetables and meats don't stick to the pan. Always use some kind of fat, just enough to coat the bottom and not so much that your food is swimming in fat.

✓ Invest in some Extra Virgin Olive Oil as well as regular olive oil. The difference is that the XV actually has a distinct flavor and is a beautiful addition when sprinkled on a finished pasta, fish, meat, vegetable or salad. Your regular olive oil will be used on direct heat, whereas your XV is generally not heated much. That's a very simplified, unscientific answer, and it's all you really need to know.

✓ Bacon fat is *not* garbage! When you cook your bacon on Sunday morning, reserve a container to pour in your fat and reserve it. You have no idea how delicious fried potatoes are in bacon fat. Just think of the possibilities! You can have the deep, rich essence of bacon that will enliven your pasta or rice dish without the clumsy chunks of bacon or the trouble of cooking bacon every time you want to deepen the flavor of a dish. Wait until it cools just a bit in the pan so that you don't run the risk of scorching yourself when you pour it into a container—best through a strainer to avoid catching burned speckles of food.

✓ Same goes for chicken fat (and duck fat...mmmmm)

✓ Butter acts as a thickener as well as a flavor-enhancer. When we discuss *emulsifiers* in Chapter 2, I'll show you how butter can thicken and add richness to a sauce without being a *butter sauce*. Subtle flavors, simple techniques!

Demystifying Terms

*What the heck is **Deglazing, Reductions** and **Caramelizing** and why do I need to know?*

When you watch cooking shows on TV or in reading cookbooks and hear these terms, that's when you know it's time to change the channel or pick up People magazine. Let's demystify some of these terms because they will be a lot of fun to use.

- ✓ **Deglazing**. The act of loosening cooked food bits, or "pan scrapings" with the introduction of liquid to a heated pan is deglazing, and it totally rocks.

    - ○ When you drop some shrimp in a hot pan with some oil, garlic and scallions, you'll notice that there are bits of darkened food stuck to the pan. Guess what: this isn't garbage. If you splash in a shot-size amount of white wine, stock/broth, lemon juice, or even water into that pan while the heat is still on and scrape the bits up with the back of your wooden spoon, that is *deglazing*.

    - ○ When Mom takes the turkey out of the oven and your Uncle Martin deftly lifts the bird onto the platter, you'll see delicious bits of fat, cooked onions and celery, turkey juice, meat, skin and spices caked up on the bottom. Throwing in a can of chicken broth while keeping the roasting pan on the stovetop and scraping up those bits of glossy, fatty deliciousness will result in a perfect gravy. (Ok, there's more to it, but not much more, believe me.) Mom may not use the term deglazing, but that's what she is doing.

- • **Reductions**. *Reducing* any liquid is to boil it until it starts to evaporate. When you go to a restaurant and they offer a roasted lamb leg with balsamic reduction; or pan seared scallops with a tequila-lime reduction, all it means is that the balsamic vinegar or their tequila-lime concoction has been boiled down to the essence of its flavor, thickened slightly (because most of the water has been evaporated out), and is very intensely flavored as a result. It's a concentration of the original liquid. Many French-style sauces are based as reductions of veal stock or chicken stock or beef stock. In fact, you can *deglaze* your pan with a liquid and then *reduce* that liquid to its essence as a sauce, gravy, or flavor for a soup. One of the reasons why you simmer a simple tomato sauce for a while is to cook some of the water out of the tomatoes so you get a more intensely flavored sauce. Reducing is sometimes referred to as "cooking out", meaning to boil-out or simmer-out the excess water.

- • **Caramelizing.** No, it doesn't mean that caramel is for dinner. Back in the introduction I talked about the different flavors your tongue picks out of a single food. One of those flavors is sweetness, and you can find it in just about any food. The science of cooking out excess water in vegetables, meats, sauces or soups means that you can more readily access those underlying flavors by simple manipulation with heat and liquid. When you cook a vegetable over relatively high heat by sautéing, searing or roasting, and it begins to turn brown or change texture, you are cooking out the excess water and the carbohydrates are turning to sugar, sort of. When you cook onions in a pan with some fat slowly, as they heat they will first appear translucent, then they will begin to cook more deeply and turn a sort of melty light brown. They will taste much sweeter and won't have the bite of a raw onion. It's like a whole different vegetable. But you are not actually *adding sugar*, despite the inherently sweet taste. You can achieve this with many types of vegetables on your stove or in the oven. Provide enough fat and liquid so that they don't immediately burn to a crisp or so that they do not steam or boil, and you will have beautifully caramelized parsnips, for example. Yum.

Vegetables Are Your Friend

Those weird white carrots in the produce aisle? Parsnips. Get to know your produce! That white broccoli looking thing? Cauliflower! And it is not gross, I promise you. You'd be surprised at how amazing simply sautéed cauliflower is with some onions, parmesan and tons of black pepper. I understand that Brussels Sprouts aren't for everyone, but please give them a try by cutting them in half and caramelizing them with a touch of oil over a long, slow heat in the oven or pan! Crunchy and salty and delicious. Try some interesting, new things in your salads instead of plain lettuce: Fennel, Watercress, Endive, and Radicchio all lend themselves to great salads with nuts, seeds, fruit, cheeses, and hold up to heat should you wish to throw a sliced, grilled pork tenderloin over any of the above and splash with some EV and a touch of balsamic...outstanding.

When you are cooking intuitively, remember, there are no rules. Who says you can't make a fennel parmesan? Why does it have to be eggplant? Like eggplant? Try sun-dried eggplant instead of sun-dried tomatoes tossed with your pasta along with some garlic, chives, and fresh basil.

The great thing about vegetables is that they are relatively inexpensive, they come in all shapes and sizes (and frozen, canned, dried and fresh), and are really much more versatile than you may have ever thought. Take a Portobello mushroom out of the oven after roasting it for about 20 minutes, seasoned with some olive oil, and immediately throw it into a marinade of crushed olives, smashed fresh herbs, olive oil, balsamic vinegar and red onions and maybe some other stuff, and then tomorrow after it's been sitting in the fridge in this delicious marinade overnight, you can throw this 'shroom on the grill and stick in between a toasted bun with some melted fontina cheese and you'd never know it wasn't a burger. Vegetables don't need to be boiled or steamed all the time; consider tossing them with some olive oil and seasoning and then roast them in the oven for 20 minutes or so; or grill them on a skewer on the barbeque.

The point is, explore fresh vegetables and cook them in ways you never thought possible.

Making a Lot out of a Little

Present it Nicely. Friends call and are just passing through town on a Sunday afternoon and would love to stop by to see you…in 15 minutes. It's mid afternoon and you don't want to keep them for dinner, but feel compelled to offer *something* besides wine. You have nothing fancy, in fact, you have nearly nothing and you start to panic. No time to run out to the store. You'll be fine! Grab your most exotic platter: you'll serve peanut butter sandwiches on it if you have to. But make it look good and I guarantee it will taste better!

- **Beautiful food comes from beautiful ingredients.** Don't roughly chop an old carrot and onion and randomly throw them in the bottom of your soup base pot: take some time to peel the carrot, cut off the ends, and peel off the yucky parts of the onion and take the time to chop both vegetables in about the same size. Just because they will be simmering for hours and possibly blended or pureed later doesn't mean they can't look delicious before they get cooked. I know you're in a rush! But I encourage you to take the time to "prepare your prep" as if it will all be served to the King. Your entire cooking experience will be more gratifying, and your food will taste better. Seriously.

- **Family Service vs. Individual Plates**. Depending on the size of your dinner party or family, you might want to consider plating your meal in the kitchen on the individual plates instead of having giant platters cluttering the table. The benefit is that you can control portions and control how the food looks on the plate. The drawback is that unless you have a helper or two in the kitchen, it is time consuming and food could cool off by the time you sit down.

- **Be Resourceful**. Although we would all love to have a fridge full of market-fresh, organic ingredients all the time, we don't. Sometimes all we are looking at in our pantries is a can of tuna, peanut butter, and some old rye bread. Don't despair! You would be surprised with what you can work with once you stop and give it some thought. Each year in our Christmas stockings, a few cans of completely random foods appear—Portuguese olives, diced papaya, pickled pearl onions, jalapenos, canned meats of various varieties. I surprise myself at some of the uses these fringe elements of the canned food world can provide.

- Old (but not moldy!) bread can be toasted on a cookie sheet in the oven and blended for fresh breadcrumbs; or sprinkle some butter or olive oil on the bread and toast to use as crackers for cheese and dips.

- Canned olives might be crushed and sautéed with onions and pine nuts or added to your tomato sauce

- Pickled pearl onions is a tough one—if you don't want to put it in your martini, I'd make a *mostarda* (sweet and sour chutney-type sauce) by coarsely chopping them, adding some mustard seeds, balsamic vinegar, honey, fresh rosemary, sea salt and sauté it all in a pan with some wine and let it *cook down* until the alcohol is cooked out of the wine and the sauce appears to all have cooked together. Tasty. Serve it with some roast pork or steamed vegetables.

- Diced, canned exotic fruits may appear to be scary. And before you plan your adventure in cooking with them, open the can and taste what's in there, first. Be sure to rinse them off. In a savory salad or roasted or sautéed with fish or meats can be quite tasty

Food Safety

Generally, common sense will guide you through your food safety questions. If it doesn't smell right, throw it out. If it doesn't taste right, throw it out. There are no rules. We've all pushed the envelope with that mystery container in the back of the fridge; sometimes it can contain a gem, sometimes just green fuzz. Unfortunately, lack of food safety training has led to too many cross-contaminations and food poisoning incidents in the home. Nothing reminds me more of this nightmare than when my grandmother stuffed the turkey with sausage stuffing and didn't cook it enough and the whole family got sick. Yuck.

Checklist to avoid such unpleasant experiences with food include:

✓ Scrub your cutting board and knife with warm, soapy water in between usage, especially when handling raw meat or fish before/after vegetables

✓ Don't forget to wash your hands with that warm, soapy water in between handling raw meat! You can't be careful enough

- ✓ Let raw meat defrost in a deep dish or bowl on the bottom shelf of the fridge, so that if anything drips, it can be wiped off and won't drip into other foods

- ✓ Cold cuts go bad pretty fast, and you might not taste the 'off'. Listeria is a bad bacteria and cultivates freely in cold cuts when kept at the wrong temperature or when too old.

- ✓ This may seem like a no-brainer, but wash your vegetables and fruits in cool water, and use a vegetable brush (you can buy one anywhere—it is not the same, however, as a scrub brush!). Rinse your meat under the cold water in an empty sink when you remove it from the packaging from the store.

Quick tips

Some tips that have made my life easier include:
- ✓ Before you open your fridge, do the dishes in the sink, first. This means that when you are finished cooking your big (or small) meal, you won't have double the dishes sitting in the sink. You want to keep a clean, organized area so that you don't spend time looking for your peeler when your pan on the stove is heating up to the point of melting.

- ✓ Get a small set of kitchen bowls. They can be a graded set of small bowls, or the same size. But they are very, very helpful when you are putting your "mise-en-place" together before you start cooking. You can lay everything you need out beforehand, in nice, tidy matching bowls!

- ✓ Put a damp cloth or paper towel underneath your large cutting board to keep it from slipping across the counter

- ✓ Use a damp cloth to keep a bowl from slipping as you're whipping or mixing ingredients: fold it lengthwise and wrap around the bottom to serve as a brake to keep the bowl from spinning as you spin your whisk

- ✓ Some fresh herbs can be frozen for a short time to preserve their vibrant flavor. I've done it with basil (beware, it looks ugly once frozen, but still tastes great), sage, thyme, rosemary, tarragon (not so good, but it works), oregano, marjoram, chervil (not so good but it works)

- ✓ If you're afraid of over-seasoning, start with just a little, then keep tasting as you continue to add little by little. You can always add, but you can't take the salt out of a sauce!

✓ Speaking of over-seasoning, the most common questions I get are around the theme of, "my soup came out too salty, how do I fix it?" You don't. There is absolutely no cosmic answer to that question, other than the option of diluting it with water to dissipate the taste of the salt. It's not hard to fix, it's just not how you planned it would be—so stay flexible and let your intuition will guide you through your soup!

Random piece of information for real beginners: boiling water?

For any beginners who are confused about foods to be cooked in boiling water, here's a guide:

- Rice goes in unboiled water: 1 part rice, 2 parts water, bring to a boil, then cover and lower heat to very very low.
- Potatoes go in unboiled water: for boiled, mashed, whatever, don't boil the water first for your potatoes. (The water will scald the outer part of the potato and it will come apart leaving you less potato to work with.)
- Pasta goes in boiled water. Period.

Chapter 2:   Start from the Start

Vinaigrettes and Marinades

Playing with food can be like a science project in some instances. This is especially true when making a vinaigrette for a salad or as a sauce. Some beautifully integrated vinaigrettes are simple *emulsifications* of fats and liquids. The science here is that you **can** mix oil and water! The art, of course, is making it taste good. The key is to use an *emulsifier* to integrate the two categories using friction and/or heat. Emulsifying ingredients may include mustard, mayonnaise, honey, egg, or ketchup, but the list goes on. These ingredients assist in integrating the oils of the world with the waters of the world. Emulsification can also be achieved using heat and friction, as in a white-wine-butter-glaze. No need to go into that now.

Just slapping together oil and vinegar may not make the cut, especially if you've prepared an interesting salad. And even if you have a really boring salad, it would become more interesting if you had a tasty, emulsified dressing. You'd be surprised that honey and/or sugar, or sweet juices added to your oil and vinegar make a fantastic vinaigrette.

The key is to create an emulsifier to integrate the two categories using friction and/or heat. The simplest way to make the simplest last-minute salad dressing without opening a preservative-laden store brand is...

Simple salad dressing

- ✓ Wrap your bowl with your dampened cloth to keep it from slipping

- ✓ Place your cutting board over a dampened cloth or paper towel

- ✓ Take out your whisk and a sharp chef's knife

- ✓ Finely chop about a half small red onion

- ✓ Assemble your mise-en-place in small, separate bowls:

- ✓ Finely chopped red onion (about 1 tablespoon)

✓ Mustard or mayonnaise (about 2 teaspoons)

✓ Honey (about 2 teaspoons)

✓ Your preferred vinegar (about ¼ cup)

✓ Olive oil or your preferred salad oil (consider grapeseed oil!) (about 1/3 cup)

✓ Salt and Pepper

✓ Place all ingredients except your oil in the bowl.

✓ Slowly add the oil with one hand as you whisk everything together quickly with the other. (Remember, your bowl will not slide away because you've secured it with the damp towel so you can use both hands to work your ingredients.)

✓ Once you've emulsified your ingredients—you'll notice how the vinaigrette is thickened and does not separate—you can begin to season it.

✓ Add some salt and pepper. Taste the mixture and re-season, if necessary. Remember, this is going to dress a salad, so it should have a zing to it, but not an overwhelming dose of vinegar or salt or sweetness.

✓ If you taste too much sweet, or too much acid, or if there's not enough "bite" (generally means it needs more acid=vinegar) and is too oily. Adjust these flavors, you know how to do it, just listen to your tongue! The re-season with salt ensuring you've balanced these flavors.

This is the basis for just about every vinaigrette I've made. You can swap out different flavored honeys, vinegars and infused oils; or change up the mustards if you use different mustards. Remember the science, too: the purpose of the vinegar is that "bite," and it can be achieved with another acidic liquid, like lemon juice or lime juice or grapefruit juice. (These are *acidic* juices, so don't make salad dressing with prune juice or Gatorade, they are not acidic enough to achieve that "bite" that a stronger acid would achieve).

You might notice that when you go to some restaurants, there are various chilled sauces squirted or zig-zagged across your plate. These are often *emulsions* of different flavor bases, meaning that there is a blend just like in the *Basic Salad Dressing*. You could use any number of flavors to emulsify into a light sauce, vinaigrette or marinade. Here are just a few examples:

- **Porcini Mushroom-Balsamic**:
  - Using the technique in assembling a simple vinaigrette in blending together a Porcini mushroom water (this is the strained water you've used to re-hydrate your dried porcinis) and XV with Balsamic vinegar, you will need to introduce a light mustard and some honey to help the ingredients emulsify.
  - This might be nice as a dip (can be thickened with white bean puree, or with cream cheese or sour cream, or if you puree the mushrooms themselves), or served over London broil, or over sautéed vegetables
- **Beet Vinaigrette**:
  - You'll use freshly roasted and peeled beets (time consuming! otherwise, opt for a good quality canned beets, preferably whole) and crush them in your cuisinart or blender with some red onion and/or scallion, XV, and the vinegar of your choice with a small squirt of mustard. For a lighter vinaigrette with the same flavor, use the water from the bottom of the roasting pan you used to cook the beets instead of the whole beets themselves. Just remember to season this aggressively!
  - In general, I wouldn't use a beet vinaigrette on a beet salad. Use your beets for something else...You want to offer some different flavors, to set off the ingredients. I would use a beet vinaigrette with a bean salad, or with an endive salad. The sweetness of the beets is a good counter to the bitterness of those greens. Plus, the fantastic color of this sauce looks great on white vegetables, or sprinkled around the plate of sliced chicken.

- **Carrot-Ginger Sauce**:
  - Clean your carrots and slice them in pieces so that they will be pureed effectively. Buy fresh ginger—it looks like a knotty root in your produce section—and peel the skin off the small section you would like to use with a paring knife, and chop it well. Put these ingredients in your blender with a touch of sesame oil, rice wine vinegar, and a little bit of soy sauce. The carrots may not be as sweet as you would like, so have some raw sugar to add little by little as you blend. Remember that when blended, you may be quite far off from the flavor you want, so have some more ginger, sugar, vinegar on hand in case you need to add more. This sauce is a particularly stubborn one to achieve greatness with—so be patient

and keep manipulating the flavors, but it is gratifying!

- o Serve this over iceberg or romaine lettuce; or over steamed vegetables and rice; or with tofu; or over thinly sliced beef or pork.

- **Roasted Garlic and Apple:**
  - o Roasting garlic is a beautiful thing. Either peel a bunch of cloves, or buy the pre-peeled cloves. Never buy the minced garlic in jars—it is bitter and contains preservatives and acidic additives which drastically change the flavor. Plus, for this recipe, you can't roast minced garlic.
  - o Keep the cloves whole and roast them in a shallow pan in the oven with a squirt of some liquid with a foil top. Depending on your flavor preference, you could use sweet vermouth, chicken stock, balsamic vinegar or something else. Roast them until they are soft and browned all the way through, but not to the point where they are hard and crusty.
  - o Peel and cut up an apple
  - o Add garlic, apple and a touch of mustard, XV, vinegar, honey and blend!
  - o Enjoy this sauce on everything. Mix it with pureed beans, pour it on rice, salads, flavor a bland soup, marinate a pork loin!

Cold Salads and other uses for Greens and Lettuces

Wake up from your bland, same-old-same-old salad doldrums! Get used to fruits, nuts, seeds and cheeses mingling intimately with your greens. And most of all, throw away those store-bought dressings. With beautiful and innovative ingredients, sometimes you won't even require the extra flavor boost of a dressing.

First, choose pristine lettuces. Everyone loves their iceberg and bottled ranch dressing, but that's not what you picked up this book to accomplish (although I do have a great way to make your own ranch dressing which is much more interesting). If you buy a mesclun mix, prior to serving it, be sure to pick through and remove the nasty, black mushy leaves. They are gross and no one wants that on their plate. It's worth your time.

Ranch Dressing

In a blender, put the following in:

4 egg yolks separated

Separating eggs: Wash your hands! Get a clean bowl separate from the one you're making your dressing in and set it in a clean sink. Crack an egg over the bowl slowly. Hold the egg in your hand and let the "white" slip through your fingers into the sink, and down the drain! Now you're holding a yolk. Drop the yolk into your bowl.

1 small peeled garlic clove

1 Tablespoon of Cider Vinegar

1 scallion chopped finely

Blend away! Then slowly pour in:

Your favorite salad oil

Taste the concoction, and adjust using the following:

Salt, Pepper, Sugar

Explore your produce aisle for other leaves and vegetables that you can eat cold and raw. I love **boston lettuce** instead of romaine with a creamier dressing. **Arugula** is a wildly versatile leaf that can withstand a good wilting underneath a grilled hangar steak or chicken breast. **Baby spinach** loves hanging out with nuts, fruit, bacon, onions and goat cheese.

But salad doesn't only mean lettuce. One of my favorite vegetables is **fennel.** If you slice fennel thinly or by using one of those cool *mandolines*, it is a juicy and refreshing vegetable and is extremely versatile in salads.

Frisee is a lot of fun and looks beautiful on the plate. It works well with light vinaigrettes rather than the thicker emulsions and also holds up to heat, as well.

Endive and others in its family of bitters include treviso, radicchio, and chicory. Because of their natural bitterness, they work incredibly well with bold, sweet additions like fruit and balsamic vinegars; and/or set off with strong cheeses like **gorgonzola, ricotta salata** or **sharp cheddar.**

Try some of these ideas with your salad greens with...

- grapefruit (or orange), red onion, pecans
- bleu cheese and grapes
- walnuts, roasted and sliced scallions, tomatoes

Get to know your **seeds and nuts** to drop into salads. I love sunflower seeds (the seedless seeds), or toasted and seasoned pumpkin seeds. Caraway seeds are great, as well. There are plenty of others to experiment with. As is the case with many nuts and seeds, a light toasting in a closely-watched pan for a few minutes to release the *essential oils* will undoubtedly enliven the natural flavor. And remember to use some of your toasted *croutons* from your stale bread—break up the pieces and put in a bag with seasonings like herbs, or ground cumin, salt and pepper.

Other chilled salads that are not predominantly raw, leafy vegetables may include pastas, beans, *blanched* vegetables, and meats or fish. These are wonderful additions to a barbeque instead of the run-of-the-mill mayonnaise-based potato and macaroni salads.

Potato Salad...LOSE THE MAYO (or at least make the aioli on your own – blend an egg yolk with salt and slowly drizzle in very high quality extra virgin olive oil until and a little mustard)

My favorite way to make a potato salad is to dump a ton salt and pepper, herbs or a loud spice like turmeric or coriander, sliced scallions or chives, and lots of tasty vinegar and XV just after you drain your cooked, sliced potatoes out of the boiling water. This way, the potatoes absorb the flavors. Serve it at room temp or chilled, and you don't have to worry about the nasty mayonnaise giving everyone botulism!

Snacks, Appetizers, Party foods

As much as everyone in the world loves little fried things and pigs in a blanket, it is not the only thing you must serve at your cocktail party. Bite-sized snacks are a bit time consuming, but creating them on your own is more fun and much less expensive. And remember— fried things are really only good once they're out of the fryer...not once they've been sitting around or reheated—that goes for mini-crabcakes!

One thing to note is that if you are having a cocktail party or just need to put out snacks rather than a meal, consider that you can use side-dish-type foods with small plates and forks instead of just finger foods. When you're scrounging for a last-minute hors d'oeuvre, just make sure it's something you would eat if someone served it to you. Seriously.

- ✓ Buy that weird brown bread in the supermarket and spread it with a mixture of cream cheese and butter and put some smoked fish on it. Cut the bread up in quarters. Sprinkle something green over it—parsley, dill, any fresh herb.

- ✓ Take your favorite canned beans—**cannellini** are my favorite—and puree them with some XV, lots of salt, a little red onion and/or scallion, a splash of your favorite vinegar, pepper and serve as a dip.

- ✓ Take another of your favorite beans and let them sit in a bath of chopped fresh herbs, XV, salt, pepper, splash of vinegar and serve with crackers or chips

- ✓ Baked cheesy-poofs.

  - o Grab some frozen pastry dough from the market. Follow the directions (not letting it thaw too much because it is hard to cut and shape). Cut into foldable shapes, maybe about 1 ½" (squares, large triangles)

  - o Also grab your favorite soft cheese—I prefer goat cheese, but you can use a combination of most cheeses. Or use cream cheese and season it.

  - o Chop some fresh herbs and mix in with the cheese, softened to room temp. Add some scallions and some cracked black pepper.

  - o Drop a small dollop of the cheese mixture onto a little squares of the pastry dough, close it up triangular shaped and bake until brownish.

Awesome.

- o   I also saute mushrooms with onions and seasoning and finely chop that mixture up and add it to fresh ricotta or goat cheese and use that on the dough.

✓   Make a giant bowl of roasted vegetables and season them well. Cut the vegetables (zucchini and other summer squashes, sweet potato, cauliflower, red onion, yellow pepper) into larger-than-bitesize pieces.

- o   They can be served at room temp with crusty bread, and make a spread or a dip that can be made from the pureed beans, above, or from pureed sundried tomatoes, XV, vinegar and herbs.

✓   Broil or grill a London broil (or roast a beef) that you've marinated for a day or so in red wine, XV, herbs, or a southwestern rub (coriander, cumin, cayenne, paprika). Let it cool, or cook it a day or so ahead, and slice it thinly. Serve it over toasts, or just spread out nicely with some chopped parsley.

- o   Use a "dipping" sauce—a *salsa verde* of sorts—like blanched, pureed parsley and other fresh herbs (basil, chervil, tarragon) blended with XV, salt and pepper, or add mayonnaise…if you must!

✓   Old bread can be your friend. Cut off crusts and arrange on a baking sheet. Sprinkle some olive oil and salt on the bread and put in the oven for a few minutes until well-toasted through. Instant bruschetta bread!

- o   Use the bread for dipping or accompaniment, or

- o   Finely dice some tomatoes, garlic, parsley and let soak in a tasty bath of salt, pepper, XV and a splash of vinegar

✓   Cooked lentils (or other beans) tossed with that same tasty bath of garlic, parsley, salt, pepper, XV and a splash of vinegar

✓   Finely diced red, yellow and orange peppers…you got it, in that bath!

✓   Finely diced sautéed mushrooms and onions…bathed in flavor, as discussed above!

✓   Mini-meatballs rock everyone's world. You can serve this with marinara, or a sweetened sauce (sounds gross, but dump some grape jelly, ketchup into a little of that marinara and you have "sweetish meatballs"). You can roast these babies or fry them in a pan.

- ✓ Get a mixture of ground beef, pork and veal from your butcher in the grocery store

- ✓ Mix it with lots of salt, pepper, ground parmesan, some seasoned breadcrumbs, and a handful of fresh chopped herbs. I like to put in pignoli (pine nuts) and chili flakes, too.

- ✓ **Before you begin rolling into shape and baking or frying, take a bit of the meat mixture into a hot pan and cook it to sample the flavor. Does it taste ok? If not, re-season, and then re-cook to re-taste!

- ✓ Here's a ridiculously simple last-minute platter of snacks:

- ✓ Cut up **apples, pears** and sprinkle some **walnuts** and **honey** over the nicely arranged platter. If you have some **salami**, **olives**, **dried fruit**, or some mystery meat in a can, arrange that on the platter as well!

Chapter 3   Uncovering the Mystery of Soups, Sauces

Life Without Cans

People in general like soup. There is little need for canned soup, now that you are an intuitive cook! When you open your mind to the endless possibilities of soups and sauces that you can make on your own without the preservatives and sugars and sodium and industrial ingredients you will find in prepared and canned soups.

You can make your own chicken broth and vegetable broth, very easily. There are packaged ones that are ok, but again, you have to watch out for the amount of sodium and preservatives. Just buy a tasty chicken (of course I recommend a free-range organic!) , put it in a large enough pot to cover with water, and throw in some bay leaves, carrots, onions and celery and simmer for a couple of hours. Strain the liquid and season it. You can put it in an ice tray in the freezer so that you have easy access to your stock and it can be stored for a lonnnnnng time.

Same goes for a vegetable stock. Saute a TON of vegetables and mushrooms in a bit of olive oil, with plenty of herbs, salt, pepper and bay leaves. Pour in some water and let it cook down for a couple of hours. Strain the stock and season it to store in the fridge for a couple of days or in the freezer.

Soup Base and Thickeners

There are blended/pureed soups, and there are brothy or stewy soups with chunks, vegetables, pasta or rice in them. Let's start with pureed soups. Most soups that you may associate with creamy textures need not have cream, milk or butter in them, though!

A soup base is the basic ingredients you'll use to make an array of pureed soups. Onions, celery, carrots, and a little bit of olive oil form the basis for these soups. I like to have at least as much onion as I do celery and carrot together. You will chop these ingredients neatly and nicely, eventhough you know you will be pureeing it later. Saute the ingredients in a large pot together with some salt and pepper, to help let some of the water cook out of the vegetables. Once they've become translucent after a few minutes of cooking, you can begin to add the rest of what you intend on putting in your soup. Drop in a bay leaf, too!

Pureed soups can get that creamy texture from potatoes. Leftover mashed potatoes can also do the job! It doesn't have to be a potato soup, necessarily, to use potatoes as a thickener. You can use an array of vegetables as your soup:

- Fennel
- Mushroom
- Parsnip
- Beans
- Carrot (probably won't need potato)
- Beet (probably won't need potato)
- Red, yellow or orange peppers (probably won't need potato)
- Celery root, turnip, rutabaga, kohlrabi and other funky root vegetables

Just cut up your soup ingredients, let it sauté and *caramelize* with the soup base, and then pour in some water, vegetable broth or chicken broth. Let it cook until all your ingredients are soft.

You can include peeled potatoes into the stage when you pour in the liquid. You'll have to manage the amount—I'd forecast that 2-3 potatoes for a 2-carrot, 3-celery, 3-onion soup base, but use your judgment.

Now comes the fun part! If using an immersion blender, turn off your heat and take the pot off the stove and place on a secure surface near a plug. Blend until your heart's content! If using a blender or cuisinart, try to let the soup cool a bit before blending and use a cup with a handle or a small ladle to move the soup ingredients from the pot to the blender. Use less than more to avoid scalding yourself! Have a large storage bowl or another pot ready to dump in the blended soup.

If you really want to get fancy, you can strain the blended soup in a *chinois* or a fine strainer for a very creamy consistency. I often opt out of this! But in any event, check the thickness of the soup. You may have to add some water or more stock to thin it out. If it is already too thin, don't despair. Just boil another couple of potatoes and add to the soup for more blending. Remember, at each step, re-seasoning is important.

Now comes for the seasoning. This is the most important part of your soupmaking pursuit. Have on hand a some of these seasonings to balance out your soup and give it some flavor:

- Honey
- Sugar (brown, refined, turbinado)
- Balsamic vinegar, flavored vinegars, cider vinegar
- Lemon juice, citrus rinds
- Parsley, mint and other chopped herbs
- Salt, pepper, and other spices (cumin, paprika, cayenne, star anise, coriander, ginger, and tons of other great stuff!)

Carefully adding little by little and stirring to integrate, taste as you go along. This is the most time consuming part of your soup, but it is the cornerstone of a tasty soup. You don't add these seasonings to emphasize their flavor, you add them to bring out the flavors in the soup. These are subtle seasonings to balance out the flavors. To enhance or to change the flavor, you can add more to make it a carrot-ginger soup instead of a roast-carrot soup, or an orange-turnip soup instead of a turnip-potato soup! But use caution and taste often!

Usually you will have to re-season your soup after you've stored it in the fridge overnight.

The other kind of soup is a stewy or brothy one. You won't be pureeing anything for this kind of soup. Rather, you'll be dicing your soup-base (onions, carrots, celery, and maybe garlic or peppers, depending on the flavor you're going for) much smaller and prettier knowing that each piece will be found on a spoon entering your loved ones' mouths! Using the stock/broth that you've already made (or bought), you will have a cooked grain, or diced vegetables, or blanched escarole, or beans, (or all of the above!) to add. In some of these soups, I like to add a can of whole, peeled tomatoes that I've crushed by hand in another bowl. Here are some ideas for grains that can be cooked separately and added to the soup, or if you have enough liquid in the soup, cook the grains in the broth.

- Pasta: good soup shapes include ditalini, pastina and orzo
- Farro
- Wheatberries
- Barley (pearled)

So to recap, here's a **Checklist** what you have going on:

✓ Your soup base of carrots, onions, celery sautéing nicely in your large pot with some olive oil
✓ Your grains cooking in some seasoned water in a separate pot
✓ You are chopping any other vegetables to add to your soup, if needed
✓ You are tasting and seasoning as you go along!
   Now you have soup!

Stews and Sauces

Another fascinatingly easy meal you can prepare with little fuss! I just love one-pot meals. Stews can only get complicated when you don't have enough liquid to cook the meat you're using. Use only fatty-type meat, it becomes silken and delicious when cooked in flavorful liquid with onions, carrots and celery for a couple of hours! You'll use essentially the same soup base as we discussed earlier, but you're also including some heavier stuff. I do stews mostly in an Italian style, tomato-red wine-based. Brown-gravy type stews are also easily achieved using floured chunks of meat and a meat broth.

The basic tenets of a stew are:

- Soup base ingredients: onions, carrots, celery

- Meat (yes, you can go meatless!) that you have in cubes that is dredged in a plate of flour that you've seasoned with salt and pepper

   o You will *caramelize* the meat in the stew pot either before or after you've sautéed your soup base. Cook that meat until it is nearly black! That's the tasty part. Then you will dump in the liquid, below.

- You can use this recipe to *braise* a brisket or pot roast, as well

  - Broth, water, red wine, crushed canned tomatoes

    - Only use great wine! Remember, a crappy wine will *reduce* into a crappy sauce

  - Armfuls of salt, pepper, fresh and ground herbs and spices. And don't forget those bay leaves!

And that's it. Seriously. The tasty part comes from the <u>hours</u> of *stewing* that the ingredients will integrate and the flavors will concentrate. Add some potatoes towards the end because they will cook in about 20 minutes. This stew just rocks!

Here is a Checklist

- ✓ Buy a couple of pounds of "stew meat" (ask your grocer's butcher for his recommendation that day); I prefer short ribs over all, but some think it's too fatty

- ✓ Medium chop 3 carrots, (maybe even some parsnips!), 3 celery stalks, 3 onions

- ✓ Open a bottle of good red wine

- ✓ Put a plate of flour aggressively seasoned with salt and pepper

- ✓ Open and crush a large can of whole peeled tomatoes

- ✓ Heat a large casserole or giant skillet (that has a matching cover).

- ✓ Dredge your meat chunks in the flour. Dump the rest of the flour (do not reuse!) and save plate

- ✓ When the pan is hot, pour in just enough oil to coat the bottom then put meat in and allow to brown very dark. Turn when very brown to allow all sides to brown.

- ✓ Remove meat and reserve on plate. Replenish oil, if necessary (probably not) and put your vegetables in the pan to caramelize. Once done, put the meat back in.

✓ Deglaze your pan with the wine first. Pour in about a little less than ½ the bottle. Let the mixture come to a boil and simmer down for a while, just a few minutes, while you are scraping all the brown cooked parts off the bottom of the pot.

✓ Once the alcohol has cooked out of the wine, drop in the tomatoes and cover the pot and lower the heat, using a handful of herbs, bay leaf, salt and pepper. Let this cook for a couple of hours!

✓ Serve alone, or with potatoes that you've put in during the last 30 min of cooking or so, or over buttered wide egg noodles. Soooooooo good.

Thickeners

Soup thickeners can be potatoes, as we discussed, and can also be bread and breadcrumbs, or even cooked or canned beans prior to pureeing. You can also set some old crusty bread in your brothy soup overnight for what the Italians call a *ribollita*, which is a soup thickened with bread and *not* pureed.

Butter can be used as a thickener, but only subtly. Cream is a thickener as well, but now you're talking about another flavor altogether.

A **rue** may be what you're looking for if you're cooking a clam chowder, for example. **Rue** is just butter and flour cooked slowly over a medium-low heat for a while until the floury taste is cooked out. You can then add milk to this for a *white sauce*, or add the concoction to your soup and it will thicken on its own. I use this *white sauce* to make baked macaroni and cheese by adding a bunch of cheddar cheese and American cheese and dumping it on elbow-shaped pasta. Totally delicious.

An absolute last resort is cornstarch. Yuck. But it works. But be wary, it can be wily! You need to dissolve cornstarch in liquid (preferably water), and then heat it to a boil before it has a thickening effect. Not my favorite, because it does nothing for the flavor and can over-thicken something in the blink of an eye.

Pasta Sauce

No need to ever buy a can or bottle of prepared spaghetti sauce, ever again! So simple you won't believe it. No explanation even needed! For a one pound box of pasta:

- 2 large (16 oz.) cans of whole peeled tomatoes. Dump them into a large bowl and crush with your hands.
- small handful of peeled garlic cloves
- 1 large onion, chopped
- 1 large spoonful of dried marjoram, thyme, or oregano
- 1 spoonful of sugar, or else use 1 carrot grated finely
Saute your onions and garlic in olive oil until translucent, then pour in herbs, sugar or carrot, then your tomatoes. Bring to a boil then lower heat and stir occasionally for about an hour. Season with lots of salt and pepper.

You're done. Next chapter.

No "Sauce" Needed

When you're making a pasta that you don't want to use a thick marinara for, you have a million options. Don't be concerned that there is no "sauce" pre-prepared. Here's an example:

If you have some shrimp, focus on cooking the shrimp, throw in some white wine and let that cook out, a handful of parsley and maybe some sliced sundried tomatoes

When the pasta is done, combine it with the shrimp and reserve some of your cooking liquid from the pasta, or use some chicken or vegetable stock on hand to "lubricate" and serve as a coating for the pasta. You're essentially letting the pasta finish cooking in the flavored liquid you've made of shrimp, herbs, sundrieds, wine, and stock.

To put it over the top, throw in a knob of butter and stir rapidly. There's your sauce. Whammo.

The point here is that butter can thicken your sauce, which you've made with a combination of vegetables, nuts, meat, or just herbs and/or garlic and oil. Reserving a bit of the pasta's cooking liquid also adds substance to your sauce, once you stir and finish with some XV and a handful of freshly grated parmesan cheese.

Gravy

Ha, this is a funny one. What exactly are you doing with your gravy? There are two approaches. If you've bought a pre-roasted chicken from the grocery store, for example, and would like some gravy with it, that's a simple thickened chicken stock. If you're talking about that you've roasted the chicken (or other meat) yourself, then you have a roasting pan full of juices, some vegetables, and the crusty tasty parts stuck to the bottom.

Thickening a flavorful chicken broth with any of the methods above (I suggest the rue) will work.

The other gravy is much better. You'll remove your meat and rest the roasting pan on your stovetop. Have some liquid ready—some stock/broth, or water, or even wine—and a good spatula for scraping the bottom. Put the heat on very, very low under the roasting pan and protect your hands with mitts or a dry kitchen towel. Add some liquid, little by little, scraping every bit of burned flavor from the bottom and sides of the pan. When this has boiled down a little bit, carefully empty it into a large bowl or pot to blend using your immersion blender, or into your blender.

Season, if needed, and that is one kick-ass gravy.

Chapter 4   Dessert

As I wrote earlier, I am not going to attempt to confuse you with baking recipes. There are plenty of excellent resources out there for you should you wish to begin your foray into baking. However, dessert doesn't have to be cake, and your world of desserts can certainly be simple, elegant, comforting and delicious without measuring grams of flour. This chapter is just to provide you with some ideas that you may not have come across.

- ***Frozen or pre-prepared pie crust isn't taboo.*** Absolutely use it if you find a brand you like! I happen to enjoy the challenge of making a pie crust from scratch, simply because I don't have it in my blood to naturally make a decent pie crust. So I try and try again…. Here's my most successful crust, which can of course be prepared and frozen ahead of time:

    - *Put 1 ¼ cup flour, 1 ½ stick butter in your food processor and pulse about 20 seconds until it looks granular.*

    - *Add 2 Tbs sugar, and then slowly pulse in 2-3 Tbs ice cold water. Don't ask me what the hell the cold water does, like I told you, I'm not a natural with pie crusts.*

    - *Take the dough out of the processor and ball it up in cellophane, refrigerate for a half hour or so, then roll out.*

    - *Good luck.*

- ***Frozen puff pastry is your friend***. Don't ever bother to make it from scratch. But find a fabulous, and probably expensive, brand of puff pastry and your dessert (and appetizer) days will be fruitful and prosperous. Here's an example of what is to come:

    - *Peel, core and slice a few green apples or pears or peaches*

    - *Heat an oven-proof sauté pan and add a lot of butter and sugar. Caramelize it until a dark, golden beautiful nutty brown. Do not taste with your fingers, it will burn your skin off…*

- Add the fruit to the caramel and cover the entire pan with the frozen puff pastry, folding the edges into the pan. Make sure none is coming over the sides of the pan.

- Put pan in pre-heated oven for about 10 minutes or until the pastry crust is golden and "puffed." While it is cooking, find a plate or serving dish that is flat and larger than the pan, because you will be turning over your apple tart onto the plate. Be careful not to burn yourself with the dripping deliciousness of the caramelized butter!

- Serve with vanilla ice cream or whipped cream or crème fraiche

- **Never underestimate the power of frozen fruit.** They must, of course, be doctored: *macerate* in liqueur and/or sugar, poach them in syrup. I believe one of the most fantastic and simple desserts on the face of the earth is:

  - Heat frozen raspberries in a saucepan

  - Serve over Haagen Dazs (technically I'm not endorsing any brand, but c'mon, there's not much better store-bought vanilla ice cream than that one)

  - Have seconds.

- **Speaking of fruit over ice cream**... You can poach fresh or dried fruit in sugar syrup that you can infuse with flavors. Simple Syrup is just equal parts water—or any other interesting liquid—heated to melt sugar. Red wine, white wine, port, vin santo or other sweet dessert wine, can all be added to the liquid part of the simple syrup. Drop in some fruit—berries, pears, or dried fruit.

- **Make a custard.** The only part of this equation that can be complicated is the idea that once you begin messing around with eggs on the stove, you run the risk of scrambling them...even if they are mixed in with milk, cream, sugar, vanilla, and/or marsala wine. So here are some simpler recipes to help you enjoy a custard without messing it up too much!

  - **Zabaglione** Take 5 eggs and beat them silly with ½ cup sugar in a heat-resistant bowl. Put bowl over small pot of boiling water. Continue to beat the mixture while you slowly pour in 2 cups of cream or milk, and/or marsala. This

41

is zabaglione and it totally rocks your world.

○ ***Crème Anglaise****. Any combination of cream/milk, eggs, and sugar with an orange or lemon zest, or vanilla, or cinnamon, or cardamom...flavoring is a perfect custard. Heat your 2 cups of milk or cream on the stove. Meanwhile, beat 4 eggs with your flavoring and ¼ cup (or a little more) sugar. When the milk is heated through and not yet boiling, take it off the heat and spill about 2 tablespoons into the egg mixture and beat constantly. Slowly add milk to the egg mixture, a couple of tablespoons at a time. Be patient—the reason why you're not dumping it all in is because the heat of the milk will cook the eggs...hence, a scrambled custard which is really gross. Take your time, I promise it will be worth it. When roughly ½ to 2/3 of your milk mixture is added to the eggs and no scrambling has taken place, combine the mixture back into the saucepan on a low heat and stir constantly until a thickening begins. Take it off the heat and serve warm with fruit, or a tart or storebought poundcake...or cool it down. Outstanding..*

● ***Basic Bread Pudding****. Beat 4 eggs with ½ cup sugar. Rip up some old bread, or that loaf of soda bread from last St. Patrick's day that has been sitting in your freezer, or an old panettone that has been sitting around since last Easter...you get the point. Put your bread in a baking dish and leave in the open air for a few hours or until very stale. Add 2 cups of milk to your egg and sugar bowl, adding any flavoring you choose. I always include vanilla, even if I am going in a cardamom direction. Nutmeg, cinnamon, just go crazy. The real flavoring in your bread pudding is in the fruit or chocolate or nuts you choose to add! Pour your custard over your bread and make sure the bread is soaked. Put in your preheated oven for about 45 min-hour, and enjoy!*

43

Made in the USA
San Bernardino, CA
07 February 2015